Intermittent

For Women Over 50

Guide to Longer and Healthier Life – Boost Your Metabolism and Accelerate Weight Loss, Detox and Rejuvenate Your Body, Improve Your Physical and Mental Health

ANASTASIA GILL

The information herein is offered for informational purposes solely and is universal as so. The presentation of the information is without contract or any type of guarantee assurance.

The trademarks that are used are without any consent, and the publication of the trademark is without permission or backing by the trademark owner. All trademarks and brands within this book are for clarifying purposes only and are owned by the owners themselves, not affiliated with this document.

Contents

INTRODUCTION..6

CHAPTER 1: INTERMITTENT FASTING'S BASICS............................8

1.1 How does intermittent fasting work?...................................10
1.2 Best food choices while following intermittent fasting..........14
1.3 Is intermittent fasting safe?...17
1.4 Benefits of Intermittent Fasting...20

CHAPTER 2: METHODS OF INTERMITTENT FASTING.....................26

2.1 The 16/8 method..27
2.2 The 5/2 method..29
2.3 Alternate day fasting..30
2.4 The warrior diet...32
2.5 Eat-stop-eat...33
2.6 Spontaneous meal skipping..35
2.7 Crescendo Fasting..36

CHAPTER 3: INTERMITTENT FASTING FOR WOMEN OVER 50.............41

3.1 How To Start Intermittent Fasting?....................................42
3.2 Some Dietary Requirements With Age..................................45
3.3 Health benefits of Intermittent fasting for women...............57
3.4 When Women Should Not Fast?..62

CHAPTER 4: THE BEST APPROACHES TO LOSE WEIGHT AFTER 50.........65

4.1 Some Weight Loss Strategies..65
4.2 Beginner Exercise Programs For 50-Year-Old Women.............77
4.3 How Much Exercise Should You Get?...................................78
4.4 Best Workouts For Women Over 50.....................................80
4.5 Benefits Of Exercise For Women Over 50.............................87

CHAPTER 5: BREAKFAST RECIPES FOR INTERMITTENT FASTING.........89

5.1 Poached eggs and avocado toast...89
5.2 Avocado quesadillas 91
5.3 Mum's supper club tilapia parmesan....................................93
5.4 Avocado salad with shrimp/prawn and Cajun potato.............95
5.5 Black bean burrito and sweet potato...................................97

CHAPTER 6: LUNCH RECIPES FOR INTERMITTENT FASTING..............100

6.1 Sweet potato curry with chickpeas and spinach...................100
6.2 Grilled lemon salmon...103
6.3 The best baked potatoes...105

6.4 Vegan fried Fish tacos...106

6.5 Baked Mahi...109

CHAPTER 7: DINNER RECIPES FOR INTERMITTENT FASTING...............**111**

7.1 Mediterranean chicken breast with avocado tapenade.......................111

7.2 Vegan lentil burgers..113

7.3 Brussel sprout and sheet pan chicken..115

7.4 Crock pot black-eyed peas...117

7.5 Brocolli dal curry..118

CONCLUSION..**121**

Introduction

Fasting is the practice of going without food or water for a prolonged amount of time. It could improve your well-being depending on how it is handled. Fasting is usually undertaken for dietary, political, or religious reasons. Intermittent fasting is a common practice that involves cycling through periods of feeding and fasting. Many diets prioritize what to eat, but intermittent fasting emphasizes *when* to eat.

Intermittent fasting is where you eat during specific hours of the day. Martin Berkhan popularized this style of intermittent fasting, which is where the name comes from. Fasting for a set number of hours per day, or consuming just one meal a couple of times a week, will aid in weight loss. Scientific research also suggests that there are many health advantages with intermittent fasting. Mark Mattson, Ph.D., a neuroscientist at Johns Hopkins University, has studied intermittent fasting for around 25 years. He claims that our bodies have adapted to go without meals for many hours, days, or even weeks. Before man learned to plant, there were gatherers and hunters who adapted to survive without eating over lengthy periods. They needed to because hunting game, and collecting nuts and berries required a lot of time and commitment. It was also simpler to maintain a healthier weight 50 years earlier. "There were no phones, only T.V. programs shut off at 11 p.m.; people avoided consuming before they went to bed," says Christie Williams,

M.S., R.D.N., a dietitian at Johns Hopkins. "The portions were much lower. More citizens exercised and played outdoors, getting more exercise in general. But television, the telephone, and other forms of entertainment are now accessible 24 hours a day, seven days a week. We remain up later to watch our favorite series, play sports, and talk on the phone. We spend the whole day and much of the night sitting and snacking."

Obesity, heart failure, type 2 diabetes, and other diseases may also be worsened from consuming so many calories and doing so little. Intermittent fasting has been seen in scientific trials to change these phenomena further. Give this book a try; you will learn a lot about intermittent fasting and its tremendous benefits that can improve your lifespan and health, even when you are in your 50s.

Chapter 1: Intermittent Fasting's Basics

Intermittent fasting is a way of eating, not a diet. It is a method of planning your meals so that you get the best out of them. Intermittent fasting does not alter the eating habits; however, it alters the timing of your meals.

If you think about it, intermittent fasting makes a lot of sense. Enzymes in our stomach breaks down the food we consume and then becomes molecules in the bloodstream. Sugar and processed grains (white flour and rice) are easily broken down into sugar, which our cells use for fuel. If our bodies do not need it all, it is processed as energy in our fat cells. On the other hand, sugar will only reach our cells by insulin, a hormone produced by the pancreas. Insulin is a hormone that carries sugar into our fat cells and holds it there.

Our insulin levels will decrease during meals if we do not eat, and our fat cells will be able to release their accumulated sugar to be used as energy. If we allow our insulin levels to decrease, we lose weight. The whole point of intermittent fasting is to make insulin levels drop low enough and for long enough that fat is burned off.

Why is it worthwhile to change when you are eating?

Most importantly, it is a smart way to get healthy without being on a fad diet or severely restricting your calorie intake. In reality, when you first start intermittent fasting, you will aim to maintain a steady calorie intake. Most people consume larger meals in a shorter period. Intermittent fasting is often a healthy way to retain muscle mass when gaining weight. The predominant reason people pursue intermittent fasting is to inevitably lose weight. Perhaps notably, since it takes relatively little behavior adjustment, intermittent fasting is one of the best methods for losing unwanted weight while maintaining a healthy one. This is a positive thing, as it implies intermittent fasting falls under the category of "easy enough to perform, but significant enough to make a difference."

1.1 How does intermittent fasting work?

To understand how intermittent fasting contributes to fat loss, we must first understand the distinction between the feeding and fasted states. When the body digests and absorbs food, it is in a fed condition. The fed condition typically occurs when you start eating and lasts three to five hours as the body absorbs and digests the meal you just consumed. Since your insulin levels are elevated while you are in the fed state, it is difficult for your body to burn fat. During that time frame, the body reaches a condition recognized as the post-absorptive state, which is a fancy way of suggesting that it is not processing a meal. The post-absorptive condition continues before you reach the fasted state, which is 8 to 12 hours from your last meal. Since the insulin levels are low, it is much simpler for your body to burn fat while you are fasting.

Fasting allows the body to burn fat that was previously unavailable during the fed state. Our bodies are rarely in this fat-burning condition, and we do not enter the fasted state until 12 hours after the last meal. This explains why many people who begin intermittent fasting lose weight without altering their diet, amount of food consumed, or exercise frequency. Fasting induces a fat-burning condition in your body that you seldom achieve with a regular eating schedule. Intermittent fasting could be done in various ways, but they all revolve around choosing daily eating and fasting times. For example, you might consider eating for only eight hours a day and fasting for the rest. Alternatively, you might opt to consume just one meal a day, two days a week. There are a variety of intermittent fasting plans to choose from. According to Dr. Mattson, after some time without carbohydrates, the body's sugar reserves are depleted and begin to burn fat. This is alluded to as 'metabolic flipping' by him.

"Most Americans eat in their waking hours, but intermittent fasting is in comparison to their usual eating pattern," Dr. Mattson states. "If somebody eats three meals a day with desserts and does not exercise, they're living on some calories and are not burning their fat reserves any time they eat." Intermittent fasting functions by extending the time from when the body burns off the calories from your last meal and starts burning fat.

Lower metabolism, achy muscles, decreased body mass, and even sleep problems make it more challenging to lose weight after the age of 50. Simultaneously, losing fat, including harmful belly fat, will significantly lower the risk of major health problems, including heart attacks, diabetes, and cancer. Of course, as you get older, the chances of contracting a variety of diseases rise. When it comes to weight reduction and the risk of developing age-related illnesses, intermittent fasting, especially for women over 50, can be a virtual fountain of youth in certain cases.

A quick overview of intermittent fasting plans:

This eating style can be approached in a variety of ways. Any method can be successful, but determining which one works better for you is a personal decision.

Intermittent fasting is done in a variety of ways; some popular methods include:

- The 16/8 method
- The 5:2 diet
- Eat Stop Eat
- Alternate day fasting
- The Warrior Diet
- Spontaneous meal skipping
- Crescendo fasting

Before beginning intermittent fasting, make sure to consult your doctor. The procedure itself is easy if you have his or her approval. You may use a regular solution, which limits daily eating to one six-to-eight hour span. For example, you might try 16/8 fasting, which involves eating for eight hours and fasting for sixteen. Dr. Williams is a supporter of the everyday routine, claiming that most individuals find it simple to adhere to this pattern over time.

Another method, known as the 5:2 solution, entails eating five times a week. You only eat one 500–600 calorie meal on the remaining two days. For instance, suppose you wanted to eat normally any day of the week, you would only exclude Mondays and Thursdays, which would be your one-meal days.

Fasting over extended amounts of time, such as 24, 36, 48, and 72 hours, is not always effective and may be risky. Going for prolonged periods of time without eating can cause your body to begin storing fat as a response to starvation.

According to Dr. Mattson's study, it takes two to four weeks for the body to adjust to intermittent fasting. When you are getting used to the new schedule, you might feel hungry or irritable. However, he states that research participants who make it past the adjustment period are more likely to stick to the schedule because they feel the benefits.

1.2 Best food choices while following intermittent fasting

Water and zero-calorie drinks, including tea and black coffee, are allowed when you aren't consuming them. And "eating normally" during your eating periods does not suggest "going insane." If you fill your meals with high-calorie fast food, super-sized fried foods, and desserts, you are not going to drop weight or get healthy. Although what most nutritionists love about intermittent fasting is that it helps people eat and enjoy a wide variety of foods. Dr. Williams said, "We want people to be aware and enjoy consuming fresh, healthy food." Eating with others and enjoying the mealtime moment, she continues, adds pleasure, and promotes good health. When you choose complex, unrefined carbs like leafy greens, whole grains, healthy fats, and lean protein, you cannot go wrong.

The foods mentioned below are some of the healthiest you should include in your eating habits when following intermittent fasting.

The Intermittent fasting food list for protein include:

! Eggs

! Fish and poultry

! Seafood

! Seeds and nuts

! Dairy products such as yogurt, cheese and milk

! Soy

! Legumes and beans

! Whole grains

The Intermittent food list for carbs include:

! Bananas

! Brown rice

! Mangoes

! Berries

! Apples

! Kidney beans

! Avocado

- ! Carrots

- ! Brussels sprouts

- ! Broccoli

- ! Chia seeds

- ! Almonds

- ! Chickpeas

The Intermittent fasting food list for fats include:

- ! Nuts

- ! Avocados

- ! Cheese

- ! Dark chocolate

- ! Whole eggs

- ! Fatty fish

- ! Extra virgin olive oil (EVOO)

- ! Chia seeds

- ! Full-fat yogurt

The Intermittent fasting food list for hydration include:

- ! Sparkling water

- ! Water

! Black coffee or tea

! Plain yogurt

! Watermelon

! Cantaloupe

! Strawberries

! Peaches

! Skim milk

! Oranges

! Cucumber

! Lettuce

! Celery

! Tomatoes

1.3 Is intermittent fasting safe?

Intermittent fasting is a good option compared to long periods of fasting. This entails consuming zero or very little calories for a specified period, followed by eating normally for another set period. The 5:2 diet, for example, involves eating a normal diet for 5 days of the week and consuming a quarter of one's total calories on the other two days. Intermittent fasting and a low-calorie diet were similarly effective for weight reduction and lowering the risk of cancer, cardiac disease, and diabetes, in a report comparing the two methods. Intermittent fasting was discovered to be as easy to adopt as a low-calorie diet.

According to research focused on mouse and rat studies, fasting may protect against some diseases, like diabetes, and can delay aging. In patients being tested for blocked arteries, fasting for brief amounts of time has been linked to a lower BMI, lower rates of diabetes, and a lower risk of coronary artery disease. While limited studies have found a beneficial effect on body weight, blood pressure, and improved rheumatoid arthritis symptoms, there have been no large-scale human studies on fasting. Fasting may be risky to many people's immune systems, but people can obtain medical care when deciding whether or not to fast from time to time. Some people use intermittent fasting to lose weight, and others use it to treat chronic illnesses, including irritable bowel syndrome, elevated cholesterol, or arthritis. But intermittent fasting isn't for everyone.

Before attempting intermittent fasting (or another diet), researchers recommend consulting with your primary care doctor. Some individuals should avoid introducing intermittent fasting to their lifestyle. These include:

!   Children and teenagers under the age of 18.

!   Women who are expecting a child or who are breastfeeding.

!   People who have diabetes or other blood sugar concerns.

!   Those who have had an eating disorder in the past.

People who aren't in these groups can successfully perform intermittent fasting and continue the program for as long as they desire. It has the potential to be a lifestyle improvement that brings you many advantages. Keep in your mind that intermittent fasting may also have a variety of consequences depending on the person. If you have unusual distress, headaches, nausea, or any other symptoms after beginning intermittent fasting, consult your doctor.

1.4 Benefits of Intermittent Fasting

Intermittent fasting does more than burn fat, according to research. "Changes in this metabolic switch influence the body and the brain," Dr. Mattson says. Mattson's study was reported in the New England Journal of Medicine, and it revealed information on several health advantages related to the practice. A leaner body, longer life, and a stronger mind are among them. "During intermittent fasting, several things happen that defend organs from chronic diseases such as diabetes, heart failure, age-related neurodegenerative conditions, including inflammatory bowel disease and several cancers," he adds.

Here are some benefits of intermittent fasting that have been discovered so far in research:

Thinking and memory: Intermittent fasting improves working memory in dogs and verbal memory in adults, according to research.

Heart health: Fasting over a short period of time improved resting heart rates, blood pressure, and other heart-related measurements.

Physical performance: Fasting for 16 hours resulted in weight reduction while maintaining muscle mass in young males. Mice that were fed on alternate days had greater running stamina.

Tissue health: Intermittent fasting in animals reduced tissue injury during surgery and improved outcomes.

Obesity and Diabetes: Intermittent fasting has been found to prevent obesity in animals. In six small trials, obese adult humans shed weight by fasting intermittently. So intermittent fasting is also beneficial for humans as well.

Fasting has a lot of advantages, and fat loss isn't one of them. Intermittent fasting has a slew of advantages, including the following.

1. Intermittent fasting can make your day simpler.

Usually, an individual focus on simplicity, behavior change, and reducing stress. Intermittent fasting brings a degree of ease to a diet that you can love. You do not care about breakfast until you wake up. You take a sip of water and begin your day. You like to eat and do not mind preparing, so three meals each day was never a concern for you. However, Intermittent fasting helps you consume one less meal, which ensures you will have to plan one less, cook one less, and worry about one less meal. It makes things a little easier, something you would probably like.

2. Intermittent fasting is the code to longevity.

Scientists understand that eliminating calories will help you live longer. This makes sense from a conceptual perspective. If you are hungry, your body will find ways to improve your life. But there's a problem: who wishes to starve themselves to live longer? A person always wishes to live a long, healthy life. However, it does not seem appealing to starve yourself. The positive news is that intermittent fasting stimulates several of the same pathways that calorie restriction does in prolonging life.

To put it another way, you get the perks of living a longer life without any of the hassles of going hungry. It was discovered in 1945 that intermittent fasting increased the lifespan of mice. More recently, this research discovered intermittent fasting on consecutive days resulted in longer lifespans in humans as well.

3. Intermittent fasting can reduce the risk of cancer.

Since there hasn't been much study and experimentation on the relationship between cancer and fasting, this one is up for discussion. Early indications, on the other hand, are promising. According to a study of ten cancer patients, fasting before treatment may minimize the side effects of chemotherapy. Another research confirms this claim, one that used alternate day fasting for cancer patients and found that fasting before chemotherapy resulted in higher cure rates and fewer deaths. Finally, the analysis of various research on fasting and disease results in the finding that fasting tends to decrease cancer and cardiovascular disease risk.

4. Intermittent fasting is much easier than other diet plans.

Most diets fail not because we turn to the wrong items, but because we do not stick to the diet long enough. It is not a nutrition issue; it is a problem with changing one's habits. This is where intermittent fasting starts because, after you get over the misconception that you ought to eat all the time, it is surprisingly simple to adopt. One research, for example, discovered that intermittent fasting was a successful weight-loss technique in obese people, concluding that "participants rapidly adapt" to an intermittent fasting regimen.

On the contrary between trying a diet plan and trying intermittent fasting, I would like to quote Dr. Michael Eades below, who has attempted intermittent fasting himself.

"Diets are easy to think about but challenging to obey. Intermittent fasting is the exact opposite: it is difficult to consider yet simple to implement. Most people have discussed being on a diet. When we find a diet that relates to us, it seems that following it would be easy. However, as we get down to the details, it gets difficult. E.g., I almost always eat a low-carbohydrate diet. However, if I consider going on a low–fat diet, it seems to be easy. Bagels, whole wheat bread and jam, corn, mashed potatoes, bananas by the dozen, and other foods come to mind, many of which sound delicious. However, if I had to begin a low–fat diet, I would quickly become bored and wish I could enjoy meat and eggs. So, though contemplating a diet is easy, putting one into action over time is more difficult.

There is no way that intermittent fasting is difficult to consider. When we discussed what we were doing, people were shocked and replied, "You go without eating for 24 hours?" "I'd never be prepared to do that." However, once you get underway, it is a snap. For one or two of the three meals a day, you won't have to worry about what to eat or when to eat it. It is a wonderful feeling of liberation. Your food costs drop dramatically. And you are not mostly feeling hungry. While it is difficult to conquer the fear of going without food, nothing could be simpler once you get started."

— Dr. Michael Eades

Eventually, the convenience of intermittent fasting is the greatest motivation to pursue it. It offers a full variety of health benefits without involving a significant change in your lifestyle.

Chapter 2: Methods of Intermittent Fasting

Fasting, or the restriction of or abstinence from eating food, has been practiced for moral and health reasons since ancient times. Fasting has a long tradition, but it has recently gained popularity as a weight-loss method. There is no such thing as a one-size-fits-all approach to dieting. This is true for intermittent fasting as well. The most important thing is to choose a regimen that suits your lifestyle, fitness, and goals—something that you will continue over time. Women can, in general, take a more casual approach to fast than men. Shorter fasting times, fewer fasting days, and eating a limited number of calories on specific fasting days are possible options. If you're thinking of giving fasting a chance, you have a few choices for integrating it into your everyday routine. In this chapter, we'll go through some of the more common types of fasting and why they're good for both men and women.

Intermittent fasting is most commonly practiced in the following ways:

- ! The 16/8 method, also called a lean gains method

- ! Eat-stop-eat, the 24-hour fast once or twice a week

- ! The 5:2 diet, also called a Fast diet

- ! Random meal skipping method

- ! Crescendo method, a 12-16 hours or 2-3 days a week fasting method

- ! Warrior diet

- ! Alternate day fasting

2.1 The 16/8 method

Daily Intermittent Fasting is another phrase for this specific method. You can follow the Lean Gains intermittent fasting method, which involves a 16–hour fast accompanied by an 8–hour eating cycle. Martin Berkhan of Leangains.com popularized this intermittent daily fasting style, which is where the name comes from.

It makes no difference as to when you start the eight-hour eating period. You will begin at 8 a.m. and end at 4 p.m. alternatively; you could begin at 2 p.m. and finish at 10 p.m. What works for you is what you should adhere to. Eating between 1 and 8 p.m. could be preferable for you because it can allow you to have lunch and dinner with friends and relatives. After all, breakfast is a meal you normally consume alone, so missing it isn't a big deal.

THE 16/8 METHOD

	DAY 1	DAY 2	DAY 3	DAY 4	DAY 5	DAY 6	DAY 7
Midnight 4 AM 8 AM	FAST	FAST	FAST	FAST	FAST	FAST	FAST
12 PM	First meal	First meal	First meal	First meal	First meal	First meal	First meal
4 PM	Last meal by 8pm	Last meal by 8pm	Last meal by 8pm	Last meal by 8pm	Last meal by 8pm	Last meal by 8pm	Last meal by 8pm
8 PM Midnight	FAST	FAST	FAST	FAST	FAST	FAST	FAST

It's very simple to get into the routine of eating on this timetable when regular intermittent fasting is practiced daily. You're probably eating at the same time every day right now without even realizing it. It's the same thing with intermittent daily fasting; you learn not to eat at some hours, which is shockingly easy.

A possible drawback to this schedule is that getting the same number of calories during the week becomes more difficult when you usually skip a meal or two during the day. Simply put, it's hard to teach yourself to consume larger meals regularly. As a consequence, many people who deal with this form of intermittent fasting lose weight. Depending on the priorities, this may be a positive or negative aspect.

This is also a safe time to find out that, while if you have been practicing intermittent fasting for the past year, you are not a diet zealot. You primarily focus on developing healthy habits that control your actions 90% of the time so that you can do anything you want with the remaining 10%.

2.2 The 5/2 method

This is one of the most famous fasting practices. The 5:2 fasting system encourages you to eat regularly for five days before limiting your calorie consumption to 500-600 calories for the remaining two. This fasting approach is very adaptable; you can fast for two days of your choice. However, at least one of the non-fasting days should be included in between the two.

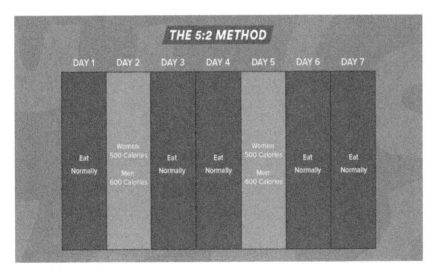

The 500 to 600 calories may be eaten in one meal or spread out throughout various meals during the day. Women who consume two meals per day should restrict themselves to 250 calories each meal, and men must limit themselves to 300 calories per meal. This method is simple to obey, particularly if you realize you are less physically active two days a week, which means you'll need to eat fewer calories for energy. When performed correctly, the 5:2 diet can be quite good for weight loss. This is due to the 5:2 eating pattern's ability to make you consume fewer calories. As a result, it is important not to overeat on non-fasting days to compensate for the fasting days.

2.3 Alternate day fasting

This diet, as the name implies, helps you to consume any other day. On Monday, for example, you will eat between the hours of 7-8 a.m. and 7-8 p.m., then fast on the Monday night and the entire day and night on Tuesday. You'd start eating again on Wednesday from 7-8 a.m., in the same order as before.

On fasting days, anyone that uses this approach can consume nutritious foods; on non-fasting days, they should eat anything they choose. This "mix-up" isn't for everybody, but it has its logic. It's better to set out time for yourself because you realize you'll be able to reward yourself afterward. Alternate day intermittent fasting requires fasting for prolonged stretches on various days of the week.

You will, for example, eat dinner on the Monday night, and then you will not eat again until Tuesday evening as shown in the graphic below. You will feed all day on Wednesday, then resume the 24-hour fasting period after dinner on Wednesday evening.

This helps you to sustain long fast cycles while also consuming at least one meal per day of the week.

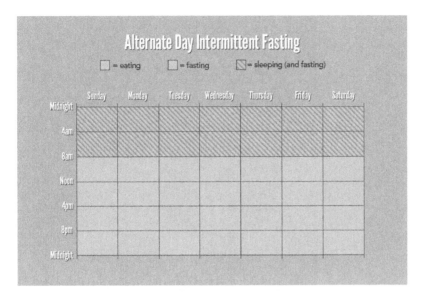

According to what most surveys have shown, this intermittent fasting method tends to be common in clinical studies, but it isn't very common in the real world. Alternate-day intermittent fasting has the advantage of allowing you more days in the fasted state than the Lean Gains process. This, in practice, would boost the effects of fasting. Hypothetically, however, you might be nervous about not eating enough. One of the most difficult aspects of intermittent fasting is teaching yourself to consume more constantly. You may be able to feast for a meal, but it requires a little planning, a lot of preparation, and consistent cooking to do so every day of the week. Consequently, most people who attempt intermittent fasting lose weight while the size of their meals stay consistent even though a few meals are skipped per week.

This isn't a concern if you're attempting to lose weight. And if you're comfortable with your weight, following the regular or weekly fasting routines won't be too difficult. However, if you fast for 24 hours a day on several days a week, it would be extremely difficult to consume sufficiently on your feast days to compensate. Consequently, most nutritionists agree that attempting regular intermittent fasting or a single 24-hour fast once a week or once a month is a safer option.

2.4 The warrior diet

Ori Hofmekler, a former participant of the Israeli Special Forces who moved into health and fitness, developed the Warrior Diet in 2001. This diet is a form of intermittent fasting, which is an umbrella term for eating habits that involve cycles of low-calorie consumption for a fixed period. The Warrior Diet is focused on ancient warriors' dietary habits, which consisted of eating nothing throughout the day and only feasting at night. The Warrior Diet is a form of eating that alternates lengthy stretches of eating less with brief periods of eating a lot. It has been promoted as a good way to lose weight, increase stamina, and gain mental clarity. A 20-hour fast is thought to be one of the old fasting methods.

THE WARRIOR DIET

	DAY 1	DAY 2	DAY 3	DAY 4	DAY 5	DAY 6	DAY 7
Midnight							
4 AM	Eating only small amounts of vegetables and fruits	Eating only small amounts of vegetables and fruits	Eating only small amounts of vegetables and fruits	Eating only small amounts of vegetables and fruits	Eating only small amounts of vegetables and fruits	Eating only small amounts of vegetables and fruits	Eating only small amounts of vegetables and fruits
8 AM							
12 PM							
4 PM	Large meal	Large meal	Large meal	Large meal	Large meal	Large meal	Large meal
8 PM							
Midnight							

This method encourages you to consume small portions of particular foods at dinner. You can also work out during dinner time. You'd have an eating window at the end of the day. While this approach is difficult to adopt, it is extremely convenient and yields incredible results. Few people choose to do so for a week or two before a big event or a photo session, but few people have the willpower to stick to it for prolonged periods. Remember that you don't have to push yourself to stick to an extreme eating schedule if it leaves you hungry and tired; pick the one that is more manageable and easier to follow!

2.5 Eat-stop-eat

A 24-hour fast is described as going without food from breakfast to breakfast, lunch to lunch, or dinner to dinner, whichever you choose. If you consume dinner at 7 p.m. on Day 1, for example, you can fast before 7 p.m. on Day 2. You may not have to fast for 24 hours, despite what the title says. You should eat one meal to tide you over and use the time to take supplements that need to be taken with meals. It is not for everybody, much like The Warrior Diet is not for everybody. If you really need to lose weight quickly, you can follow this fasting approach for a limited amount of time because it provides excellent results. It may be the day before your wedding or the day after a big Thanksgiving or Christmas meal that leaves you feeling bloated. But be smart and pay attention to your body! Moving from a complete day of feasting to a 24-hour fast can be incredibly stressful on the body. Weight reduction is one of the primary motivations for people to try intermittent fasting regimes like the Eat Stop Eat method.

EAT-STOP-EAT

DAY 1	DAY 2	DAY 3	DAY 4	DAY 5	DAY 6	DAY 7
Eats normally	24-hour fast	Eats normally	Eats normally	24-hour fast	Eats normally	Eats normally

While there are currently no studies testing Eat Stop Eat for weight loss, mounting evidence indicates that the intermittent, prolonged fasting used by Eat Stop Eat can aid many people with losing weight. Moreover, a calorie deficiency is the first and maybe the most noticeable way Eat Stop Eat will help you lose weight. It's popular knowledge that dropping weight necessitates eating fewer calories than you burn. Eat Stop Eat, when used right, sets you up with a calorie loss of 1–2 days per week. This decrease in total calorie intake will result in weight loss over time as you burn more calories than you consume.

2.6 Spontaneous meal skipping

The emphasis of random meal skipping is mostly on consuming unprocessed foods. Besides that, fasting rules are rather adjustable, and you can miss meals once or twice a week at random. Spontaneous meal skipping is a practice of listening to the body. It states that if your body does not indicate that you are hungry, you do not have to eat. The theory behind Spontaneous meal skipping is to respond to your body's cues. It supports the idea that rather than overloading your body with food excessively, even though you aren't starving, you can allow your body a pause for some time.

SPONTANEOUS MEAL SKIPPING

DAY 1	DAY 2	DAY 3	DAY 4	DAY 5	DAY 6	DAY 7
Breakfast	Skipped Meal	Breakfast	Breakfast	Breakfast	Breakfast	Breakfast
Lunch	Lunch	Lunch	Lunch	Lunch	Lunch	Lunch
Dinner	Dinner	Dinner	Dinner	Skipped Meal	Dinner	Dinner

This fasting method is ideal for busy people and those who have little time to practice various diets. It essentially assists you in reducing your calorie consumption. If you had a very heavy lunch, you might want to give your body a break and miss dinner, or at the very least eat something light, but don't overeat as you take the next meal after missing a meal. It has the potential to induce negative shifts in your body's metabolic function, which is harmful to your health. So, during your meal, make sure you consume in moderation. Make no effort to cover for the missing meal. Eat like you normally would.

2.7 Crescendo Fasting

If you're a woman, you've already heard that men have an easier time losing weight than women do. For us women, this can be frustrating! Hormone imbalances can render weight reduction

36

difficult. If you're starving yourself regularly with intermittent fasting (IF), you'll become tired and ravenous and will end up eating whatever you can get your hands on. Your body will even begin to break down your lean muscle for fuel rather than fat. So crescendo fasting is perhaps the most beginner-friendly way of fasting.

Contrary to common belief, crescendo fasting operates gently with hormones to create a balanced equilibrium, helping you maintain your appetite and stamina while still losing body fat. Fasting can occur, but in shorter, less regular bursts. This is a healthy approach to reducing your calorie intake and losing weight without putting your body in a stressful deprivation mode. After a while, you might feel more at ease fasting for longer and more regular periods. Instead of the standard IF protocol, which may have you fasting anytime from 12 to 20 hours a day, crescendo fasting reduces the fasting period to only two to three non-consecutive days a week. The word "crescendo fasting" accurately explains its goal: steadily increasing the amount of fasting the body can tolerate. So, for example, you might fast for 14 hours, beginning at 9 p.m. on Sunday and finishing at 11 a.m. on Monday. After that, you'll normally eat for the next few days before repeating the fast. It's easy and incredibly simple to execute. It often relieves a lot of anxiety if you have problems doing intermittent fasting regularly. Additionally, the body will be able to respond to longer fasts over time, allowing you to adopt a more conventional intermittent fasting schedule.

This is a simplified edition of the 16-8 technique. You choose two to three days a week to fast for 12-16 hours. The Crescendo Method is one that can be interpreted in a variety of ways. Some people believe you can fast for 12 waking hours, and others believe you should fast for a total of 16 hours. The Crescendo Method is usually used as a steppingstone into the Eat-Fast-Eat Method. Begin by fasting for 12 hours twice a week and gradually increase to 24 hours.

12-hour fast:

A 12-hour fast is described as eating for the first 12 hours of the day and then not eating for the next 12 hours. If you consume three meals a day between 8 a.m. and 8 p.m., for example, you can fast from 8 p.m. to 8 a.m. This approach is simple to execute and yields excellent outcomes in the long term.

Even though it is claimed that your body runs out of blood sugar eight hours after the last meal. It ensures that if you fast for 12 hours, you would only be burning fat for 4 hours. Of course, that's better than nothing, but keep in mind that you should start with this one, check your progress, and gradually increase your fasting period before you're able to implement the 16:8 method!

16-hour fast:

Fasting for 16 hours is a little more difficult than 12 hours, but the effects are much better. As the name suggests, you can fast for 16 hours and then eat for the remaining 8 hours of the day. While fasting this way, you must eat a lot of high-protein items and rotate your carbohydrate intake. If you work out, you can try to plan the nutrient intake carefully. This ensures that you can eat the rest of the carbs right after a workout. When you eat from 11 a.m. to 7 p.m., for example, you can eat two or four to five meals during that time and fast from 7 p.m. to 11 a.m. Any people who fast this way tend to miss the morning meal every day and still eat snacks before their other meals. This is currently the most common fasting form, and it has the best ease-of-follow and efficacy ratio!

At the end of the day, the perfect approach is something that you can handle and maintain over time without causing any negative health effects.

Chapter 3: Intermittent Fasting For Women Over 50

Intermittent Fasting may affect women and men differently. According to some reports, intermittent fasting might not be as effective for some women as it is for men. In one research, women's blood sugar regulation decreased after 3 weeks of intermittent fasting, while men's blood sugar control improved. There have also been several observational accounts about women's menstrual cycles shifting since they started intermittent fasting, since female bodies are particularly vulnerable to calorie restriction, such shifts may arise. A small portion of the brain, known as the hypothalamus, is impaired when calorie consumption is limited, such as when fasting for too long or too often. Gonadotropin-releasing hormone (GnRH) is a hormone that aids in the activation of two sex hormones: follicle-stimulating hormone (FSH) and luteinizing hormone (LH). When these hormones cannot interact with the ovaries, irregular cycles, miscarriage, poor bone strength, and other health problems may occur. While no equivalent human trials exist, 3–6 months of alternate-day fasting in female rats resulted in decreased ovary size and irregular menstrual cycles. So, women should take a modified solution to intermittent fasting, like shorter fasting times and fewer fasting days, due to these factors. As a consequence, it is advisable that you take medical guidance and consult your doctor before starting any diet.

3.1 How To Start Intermittent Fasting?

It is simple to get started. In reality, you have probably done a few intermittent fasts before. Often people eat this way out of habit, avoiding breakfast and dinner. The most straightforward approach to get started is to use one of the intermittent fasting plans listed above. You may not, though, have to stick to a strict schedule. Another choice is to fast anytime it is convenient for you. For certain individuals, skipping meals because they are not hungry or do not have time to prepare may be beneficial. It does not matter the kind of fast you want at the end of the day. Finding a tool that fits well for you and your lifestyle is the most important thing.

It is important to remember that intermittent fasting is not a diet. It is a method of eating that is scheduled. Intermittent fasting, unlike a dietary schedule that restricts where calories come from, does not prescribe which foods an individual should consume or avoid. The following tips are intended to assist women or men who are ready to begin fasting and making it as convenient and successful as possible.

1. Identify your personal goals:

An individual who begins intermittent fasting usually has a specific target in mind. That may be for weight loss, better physical health, or better metabolic function. A person's ultimate goal can help them decide the right fasting approach and measure how many nutrients and calories they need.

2. Pick up the right method:

Before undertaking another fasting method, a person can typically stay with one for at least a month. When it comes to fasting for health benefits, there are four options to consider. Women should select the plan that better fits their needs and the one they feel they will stick to. These include:

! The 16/8 method

! The 5:2 diet

! Alternate day fasting

! Eat stop eat

! The warrior diets

! Spontaneous meal skipping

! Crescendo fasting

3. Figure out the caloric needs:

When fasting, while there are no food limits, calories must always be counted. People who choose to lose weight would build a calorie deficit, which implies they must gain fewer calories than they consume. Many that wish to add weight would eat more calories than they spend. There are various resources available to help individuals estimate their caloric requirements and decide how many calories they must eat per day to maintain or lose weight. An individual may also seek advice from a healthcare professional or a dietitian on how many calories they require while following an intermittent fasting.

4. Figure out a meal plan:

Making a weekly meal schedule will assist anyone who is seeking to reduce or gain weight. A woman attempting to lose weight with intermittent fasting may find that preparing their meals for the day or week is helpful. Meal preparation does not have to be restrictive. It considers calorie consumption and ensures that the correct foods are used in the diet. Meal prep has many advantages, including assisting with calorie counting and ensuring that an individual has the necessary ingredients on hand for preparing foods, fast dinners, and snacks.

5. Make the calories count:

Calories are not always made equal. Since these intermittent fasting methods do not specify how many calories an individual can ingest when fasting, it's important that the food's nutritional content is considered. In general, nutrient-dense food, or the food with many nutrients per calorie, should be consumed. Even if individuals do not have to avoid fast food completely, they can also consume it in moderation and concentrate on healthy alternatives to enjoy the most benefits.

3.2 Some Dietary Requirements With Age

As we get older, our nutritional requirements change, and eating healthy becomes more important. Since aging is related to various changes, particularly nutrient deficiencies, lower quality of life, and poor health results, this is the case. Fortunately, you should take measures to help avoid weaknesses and other age-related shifts. Eating nutrient-dense diets and getting the right supplements, for example, will help you remain healthier as you grow older. This chapter discusses how the dietary requirements shift when you get older and how to satisfy them.

How Does Aging Affect the Nutritional Needs?

Several body changes are associated with aging, including muscle weakness, thinner skin, and lower stomach acid. As you get older, your ability to recognize hunger and thirst can deteriorate. Any of these shifts can put you at risk for nutritional shortages, while others may affect the senses and overall quality of life. According to research, 20% of older adults suffer from atrophic gastritis, a disorder in which chronic inflammation damages the cells that contain stomach acid. Low stomach acid may prevent nutrients like vitamin B12, iron, calcium, and magnesium from being absorbed.

Another issue that arises as people age is a decrease in their calorie requirements. Unfortunately, this results in a nutritional dilemma. Although consuming fewer calories, older adults need almost as much, if not more, of those nutrients. Fortunately, you may satisfy your nutritional requirements by consuming a range of whole foods and taking supplements. Another problem that people may face when they grow older is a decline in their body's ability to recognize essential senses such as hunger and thirst. Unintended weight loss and dehydration can happen as a result of this. And as you grow older, these effects can get more severe.

Needing fewer calories, but more nutrients:

The daily calorie requirements of a person are defined by their activity level, weight, height, muscle mass, and several other variables. In general, older adults require fewer calories. However, their nutritional requirements remain the same as, or higher than when they were younger. As a result, consuming nutrient-dense, whole foods becomes important. Since they walk and workout less and carry less muscle, older adults need fewer calories to sustain their weight. If you proceed to consume the same number of calories every day as you did when you were young, you are likely to gain weight, especially around your abdomen. This is especially true of postmenopausal women, as the decrease in estrogen levels during this period can stimulate the storage of belly fat.

Even if older adults need fewer calories, they still need the same or even higher amounts of some nutrients than younger people. This highlights the value of consuming a range of whole foods, such as vegetables, fruits, fish, and lean meats, for older people. These nutrient-dense foods will help you combat nutrient deficiency without adding inches to your waistline. Protein, calcium, vitamin D, and vitamin B12 are all nutrients that become more necessary when you grow older.

You can benefit from more protein:

As you get older, it is normal to lose muscle and energy. In reality, after the age of 30, the average person loses 3–8% of their muscle mass per decade. Sarcopenia is the term for lack of muscle mass and strength. It is a leading cause of elderly weakness, injuries, and poor health. More protein in your diet can help your body retain muscle mass and combat sarcopenia.

Over the span of three years, a survey observed 2,066 elderly citizens. It was discovered that those who consumed the most protein a day lost 40% less muscle mass than those who ate the least. A study of 20 recent research in older adults showed that increasing protein consumption or getting protein supplements would increase muscle mass, delay muscle loss, and improve muscle growth. Furthermore, the most successful approach to combat sarcopenia seems to be balancing a protein-rich diet with resistance exercise.

You may benefit from more fiber:

Constipation is a major health issue among older people. It is more prevalent among people over the age of 65, and women are two or three times more likely to suffer with it than men. This is because individuals in their forties and fifties appear to walk less and are more prone to take pills with constipation as a side effect. Constipation may be relieved by eating fiber. It flows through the intestines undigested, assisting in the formation of stool and the maintenance of normal bowel movements. Dietary fiber helped trigger bowel movements in individuals with constipation, according to a study of five reports.

Diverticular disease is a disorder in which tiny pouches develop along the colon wall and become inflamed or infected. A high-fiber diet can help avoid this. This is a particularly frequent ailment among the elderly. Diverticular disease is sometimes mistaken as a disease induced by a Western diet. It is very common, with up to 50% of citizens over the age of 50 in Western countries suffering from it. However, Diverticular disease is nearly non-existent in people who consume more fiber. Diverticular disorder, for example, affects fewer than 0.2 percent of the population in Japan and Africa. Increasing your fiber consumption will help you protect yourself from both this disease and constipation.

You need more vitamin D and calcium:

Two of the most essential minerals for bone protection are calcium and vitamin D. When you grow older, the body can benefit from more vitamin D and calcium. Calcium aids in the formation and maintenance of healthy bones, whereas vitamin D aids in calcium absorption. Unfortunately, older adults have a lower ability to digest calcium from their food. According to animal and humans research, the gut consumes less calcium the more we age.

However, since aging will make the body less effective at producing vitamin D, the decrease in calcium absorption is more likely due to a vitamin D deficiency. When your skin is exposed to sunlight, your body will generate vitamin D from the skin's cholesterol. However, when people age, their skin becomes thinner, reducing their capacity to produce vitamin D. These shifts can prevent you from having enough vitamin D and calcium, leading to bone loss and an increased risk of fracture. It is necessary to eat more calcium and vitamin D from foods and supplements to combat the impact of aging on vitamin D and calcium levels. Calcium is found in a variety of foods, including dark green, leafy vegetables, and animal products. On the other hand, Vitamin D could be present in several kinds of seafood, including herring and salmon. Vitamin D supplements, such as cod liver oil, may also help older people.

You may need more vitamin B12:

Vitamin B12, commonly known as cobalamin, is a water-soluble vitamin. Vitamin B12 deficiency is more common as people become older. Having a vitamin B12 supplement or eating foods enriched with vitamin B12 may be particularly beneficial to older adults. It is needed for the production of red blood cells as well as the maintenance of normal brain function. Unfortunately, studies show that 10–30% of adults over the age of 50 have a reduced ability to consume vitamin B12 from food, leading to a vitamin B12 imbalance. Vitamin B12 is bound to proteins in the foods you consume in your diet. Stomach acid will help it detach from such food proteins so the body can use it.

In older persons, disorders that decrease stomach acid output are more common, resulting in lower vitamin B12 absorption from food. One disease that may do this is atrophic gastritis. Furthermore, since vitamin B12 is more plentiful in animal foods like eggs, seafood, meat, and dairy, older persons who adopt a vegetarian or vegan diet are less likely to obtain high-quality vitamin sources. As a result, older people can benefit from getting a vitamin B12 supplement or eating vitamin B12-fortified foods. The crystalline vitamin B12 in these fortified foods is not bound to food proteins. As a result, individuals who produce lower stomach acid than average are still able to absorb it.

Some other nutrients that may help you as you age:

Other nutrients that could be beneficial when you get older include: Magnesium, potassium, omega-3 fatty acids, and iron.

53

Potassium: A higher potassium consumption is linked to a reduced risk of elevated blood pressure, osteoporosis, kidney stones, and cardiac failure, all of which are more prevalent in older people.

Omega-3 fatty acids: The main cause of death in the elderly is heart failure. Omega-3 fatty acids have been shown in studies to reduce cardiac attack risk factors such as triglycerides and elevated blood pressure. Fish is the primary provider of omega-3 fats.

Magnesium: Magnesium is an essential mineral for the human body. Unfortunately, due to medication use, inadequate intake, and age-related gut function changes, older people are at risk of deficiency.

Iron: Iron deficiency is common in the older population. Anemia, a disorder in which the blood does not provide enough oxygen to the bloodstream, can occur due to this. A diet rich in vegetables, fruits, seafood, and lean meats will provide most of these nutrients. People who follow a vegetarian or vegan diet, on the other hand, can benefit from having omega-3 or an iron supplement. While iron can be present in many vegetables, plant-based iron is not as well absorbed as meat-based iron.

You are more prone to dehydration:

Drinking lots of water becomes more important as you grow older, because your body can lose the potential to recognize dehydration. Water takes up around 60% of the body. It is important to remain hydrated at any age because the body loses water regularly, mostly through sweat and urine. Additionally, when you get older, you can become more vulnerable to dehydration. Thirst is detected by receptors located in the brain and all over the body. These can become less receptive to water changes as you age, making it more difficult for them to sense thirst. Your kidneys still help your body store water, but they also start to lose function as you get older.

Sad to say, but dehydration has serious effects on aged people. Long-term dehydration reduces the fluid in the cells, making it harder to digest medicine, causing health issues and growing fatigue. As a result, it is important to make a deliberate attempt to consume enough water regularly. If you have issues drinking water, consider getting one or two glasses with each meal. Otherwise, take a water bottle with you during the day.

You may struggle to eat enough food:

Another point of concern for the aged is a lack of appetite. If this dilemma is not solved, it may result in unwanted weight loss and dietary deficiencies. Appetite deficiency has also been related to a higher risk of mortality or poor health. Changes in taste and smell, hormones, and changes in life conditions may all contribute to a loss of appetite in older adults. According to research, older people have higher levels of fullness hormones and lower levels of hunger hormones, suggesting they may eat less often and feel fuller sooner. Researchers also noticed in a small study of 11 aged persons and 11 young adults, that older adults have slightly lower amounts of the appetite hormone ghrelin before a meal.

Furthermore, numerous experiments have reported that the fullness hormones leptin and cholecystokinin are higher in older people. Aging will impair the sense of taste and smell, leaving foods less appealing. Tooth loss, underlying illness, loneliness, and appetite-suppressing medications are also possible causes of poor appetite. If eating big meals is tough for you, consider splitting your meals into smaller pieces and eating them every few hours. Otherwise, continue and make a routine of snacking on healthy foods, including yogurt, nuts, and boiled eggs, which are high in nutrients and calories.

3.3 Health benefits of Intermittent fasting for women

Intermittent fasting is an eating practice in which a person only eats during a specific amount of time. The 16/8 process, in which you eat for 8 hours and then fast for 16, is the most common form of intermittent fasting. Intermittent fasting has been proven to help people lose weight in several research reports. Furthermore, several test-tube and animal researches indicated that intermittent fasting can help older people by extending life, preventing age-related changes in mitochondria, and slowing cell decline, the cell's energy-producing organelles. Intermittent fasting will help you lose weight while still lowering the risk of developing various chronic diseases.

Heart Health

The main cause of death in the world is heart failure. High blood pressure, high triglyceride levels, and high LDL cholesterol are the three most common risk factors for cardiac failure. In a study of 16 obese men and women, intermittent fasting reduced blood pressure by 6% in only eight weeks. According to the same report, intermittent fasting also cut triglycerides by 32%, LDL cholesterol by 25%. The evidence for a correlation between intermittent fasting and lower LDL triglyceride levels and cholesterol, on the other hand, is inconsistent.

Four weeks of intermittent fasting over the Islamic holidays of Ramadan did not result in a decrease in LDL cholesterol or triglycerides, according to a survey of 40 normal-weight individuals. Before researchers fully comprehend the impact of intermittent fasting on cardiac health, higher-quality research with more rigorous methods is still needed.

Diabetes

Intermittent fasting will also help you treat your diabetes and lower your risk of developing it. Intermittent fasting, including prolonged calorie restriction, tends to reduce many of the disease's risk factors. It mostly does this by lowering the insulin levels and decreasing insulin tolerance.

Six months of intermittent fasting showed decreased insulin levels by 29% and insulin tolerance by 19% in a randomized controlled trial of more than a hundred overweight or obese women. The levels of blood sugar remained unchanged. Furthermore, intermittent fasting for 8–12 weeks has been found to decrease insulin levels by approximately 20–31% and blood glucose levels by 3–6% in people with pre-diabetes, a disease in which blood sugar levels are increased but not elevated enough to diagnose diabetes. In terms of blood sugar, though, intermittent fasting might not be as effective for women as men. A small study showed that women's blood sugar balance deteriorated after twenty-two days of alternate day fasting, although men's blood sugar levels were unaffected. Despite this side effect, the decrease in insulin and insulin tolerance will reduce the probability of diabetes, particularly in pre-diabetic individuals.

Weight Loss

When performed right, intermittent fasting can be an easy and efficient way to reduce weight since short-term fasts will help you eat fewer calories. Several reports have shown that intermittent fasting is just as effective as conventional calorie-restricted diet plans for weight loss in the short term. Intermittent fasting resulted in an overall weight reduction of 15 lbs., approximately 6.8 kg over 3–12 months, according to a 2018 study of research in overweight adults. For 3–24 weeks, intermittent fasting decreased body weight by 3–8% in obese or overweight people, according to another study. According to the report, participants' waist circumference decreased by 3–7% during the same period.

It is important to note that the long-term consequences of intermittent fasting on female weight loss are unknown. Intermittent fasting appears to help with weight reduction in the short term. However, the amount you lose can almost definitely be determined by how many calories you consume during non-fasting hours and how long you stick to the lifestyle.

It May Help You Eat Less

Moving to intermittent fasting may help you eat less naturally. According to one report, when young men's food consumption was limited to a four-hour duration, they consumed 650 fewer calories per day. Another research looked at the impact of a lengthy, 36-hour fast on 24 active men and women's eating patterns. Despite eating more calories on the post-fast day, participants' overall calorie balance dropped by 1,900 calories, which significantly decreased.

Other Health Benefits

Intermittent fasting can also have a range of other health effects, according to a variety of animal and human reports. These include:

Reduced inflammation: Intermittent fasting has been shown in several trials to suppress key markers of inflammation. Chronic inflammation can induce weight gain and various other health issues.

Improved psychological health: In one report, 8 weeks of intermittent fasting reduced stress and binge eating habits in obese adults, thus improving body image.

Increased longevity: Intermittent fasting was also shown to extend lifespan by 33–83 percent in rats and mice. Fasting causes cells to go through an adaptive stress reaction, explaining why it has so many positive outcomes. Fasting on alternate days increases oxidative stress markers and is an indicator of longevity.

Preserve muscle mass: When compared to prolonged calorie restriction, intermittent fasting tends to be more efficient at maintaining muscle mass. And even when you are at rest, gaining more muscle mass makes you burn more calories. Intermittent fasting is likely to result in more muscle gain than most weight-loss diets. Adding exercise to the intermittent fasting plan, especially weightlifting, will help you retain muscle mass. It is, though, completely up to you whether or not you work out during fasting times.

3.4 When Women Should Not Fast?

Many women tend to remain healthy by using modified forms of intermittent fasting. On the other hand, various studies have shown that fasting days will induce hunger, mood fluctuations, loss of focus, diminished stamina, headaches, and bad breath. According to several reports on the internet, women's menstrual cycles have also been said to have ceased while on an intermittent fasting diet. Before undertaking intermittent fasting, contact the doctor if you have a medical problem. Intermittent fasting is not recommended for the following women:

! Women who have a background of eating disorders should seek medical advice immediately.

! Have diabetes or suffer low blood sugar levels daily. When you have Type 1 diabetes, you have the risk of aqcuiring excessively elevated blood glucose levels (hyperglycemia), which may lead to a build-up of 'ketones.' Ketoacidosis is a serious condition that may occur as a result of this. Passing a lot of urine, feeling very thirsty, or becoming very sleepy are all signs of elevated blood glucose levels. Speak with a healthcare provider if your blood glucose levels are elevated, and you have these symptoms.

! Are underweight, malnourished, or deficient in nutrients. The fast duration determines the changes that arise in the body during a continuous fast. Eight hours or so after the last meal, your body typically enters a fasting condition. Your body can first use glucose stored in your body, then break down body fat as the next energy source later in the fast. Using your body's fat reserves as an energy supply will result in weight loss in the long term.

! Are breastfeeding, pregnant, or trying to conceive. Fasting or starvation over an extended amount of time when breastfeeding should be ceased because it will limit milk supply, slowing the baby's weight gain over time. According to research, fasting for a short period will not affect your milk supply. And if you are not eating anything, your body can go to considerable lengths to keep producing milk for your baby. But that does not makes fasting a good choice. The nutritional content of a mother's milk is primarily determined by her diet, according to research. You absorb fewer minerals and vitamins overall when you consume fewer calories. As a consequence, milk can become less nutritious in the longer term.

! If you should conceive, IF may not be the perfect lifestyle choice for a fast-growing infant. Pregnancy necessitates a significant number of resources. Women who are pregnant need to consume more calories every day, so trying IF or staying with it during pregnancy can be placed on pause until you can speak to the doctor about it.

! Have experienced fertility issues or a diagnosis of amenorrhea (missed periods.)

That being said, intermittent fasting seems to have a favorable protection profile. However, if you have any complications, such as a lack of your menstrual period, you can quit instantly. Updated versions of intermittent fasting, on the other hand, tend to be healthy for most women and could be a safer choice than longer or tougher fasts. Intermittent fasting is something to think about if you are a woman trying to reduce weight or boost your health.

Chapter 4: The Best Approaches To Lose Weight After 50

Maintaining a healthy weight or losing extra body fat will be tough for certain people when they grow older. Weight increase over the age of 50 can be caused by unhealthy habits, a mainly sedentary lifestyle, metabolic shifts, and bad dietary choices. You are capable of losing weight at any age, regardless of your physical abilities or medical diagnoses, by making a few basic changes.

4.1 Some Weight Loss Strategies

Here are the top 19 weight-loss strategies for people over 50.

1. Learn to enjoy strength training.

Strength training is still critical for older adults, even though cardio receives a lot of focus when it comes to losing weight. Sarcopenia is a disorder in which the muscle mass reduces when you grow older. At about 50, muscle mass loss begins, which will hinder the metabolism and contribute to weight gain. After 50, your muscle mass declines at a pace of about 12% per year, while your muscle power declines at a rate of 1.5–5% per year. Using muscle-building workouts in your regimen is important for reducing age-related muscle decline and maintaining a healthy body weight.

Bodyweight workouts and weightlifting, for example, will boost muscle strength and size while still growing muscle efficiency. Physical exercise will also help you reduce weight by lowering body fat and increasing your metabolism, which will help you burn more calories during the day.

2. Team up.

It may not be easy to develop a balanced eating schedule or workout regimen on your own. Sticking to the schedule and achieving your fitness objectives can be more enjoyable if you team up with a buddy, coworker, or family member. According to studies, people who participate in weight-loss exercises with partners are more likely to keep their weight loss over time. Working out with others will help you stay committed to your fitness regimen and make things more exciting.

3. Move more and sit less.

To lose excess body fat, you must burn more calories than you consume. That is why, when attempting to lose weight, becoming more active during the day is important. Sitting at your desk for long periods, for example, can hinder your weight loss efforts. To combat this, actually getting up from the desk and having a five-minute walk every hour will help you feel more involved at work. According to studies, using a Fitbit or pedometer to watch your steps will help you lose weight by increasing the activity and calorie expenditure. Start with a rational step target focused on the current activity rate by using a pedometer or Fitbit. Then, based on your general fitness, gradually increase from 7,000 to 10,000 steps a day or more.

4. Bump up the protein intake.

It is important to have enough high-quality amount of protein in your diet, not just for weight reduction but also to avoid or reverse age-related muscle loss. After the age of 20, the resting metabolic rate (RMR), or the number of calories you burn at rest, drops by 1–2% per decade. This is linked to muscle weakness as people become older. A protein-rich diet, on the other hand, may help inhibit or even restore muscle loss. Increasing dietary protein has also been shown in several trials to help you shed weight and maintain keeping it off in the long run. Furthermore, evidence suggests that older adults need more protein than young people, emphasizing the importance of including protein-rich items in your snacks and meals.

5. Talk to your dietitian.

It may be challenging to find an eating routine that encourages weight loss while still nourishing the body. A certified dietitian will help you determine the most effective way to remove extra body fat without needing to stick to a strict diet. A dietitian will also help you lose weight by providing advice and guidance. According to studies, getting training with a nutritionist or dietician may achieve far more outcomes and benefits than going it alone, and it can even help you sustain your weight loss over time.

6. Cook more at home.

Numerous tests have shown that those who cook and consume more food at home have a better diet and are less obese than those that do not. When you prepare meals at home, you have complete control of what goes into and what remains out of your recipes. It also allows you to try fresh, healthy ingredients that have piqued your interest. Start by cooking one or two meals at home a week if you eat out most of the time, then gradually increase this amount until you are cooking at home more than you eat out.

7. Eat more fruits and vegetables.

Fruits and vegetables are rich in nutrients that are important for good health, and having them in your diet is an easy, scientifically proven way to lose weight. An analysis of ten research showed that increasing regular vegetable servings are linked to a 0.14-inch (0.36-cm) waist circumference drop in women. Another research found that consuming fruits and vegetables decreased body weight, waist circumference, and body fat in 26,340 women and men aged 35–65.

8. Hire a personal trainer.

Working with a personal trainer can be particularly beneficial for people who are new to working out. They can show you not only how to work out properly and lose weight, but how to avoid injury. Personal trainers will also encourage you to exercise frequently by making you accountable. They could even change your mind about working out. A 10-week survey of 129 adults reported that 1 hour of one-on-one personal training sessions improved fitness motivation and physical activity levels each week.

9. Rely less on convenience foods.

Eating convenience foods like fast food, sweets, and packaged foods regularly have been linked to weight gain and can hinder weight loss efforts. Convenience foods are high in calories and low in essential nutrients such as protein, fiber, and minerals. Fast food and other packaged items are sometimes referred to as "empty calories" because of this. Cutting down on convenience foods and replacing them with nutrient-dense whole foods in healthy meals and snacks is a good way to lose weight and stay healthy.

10. Find an activity that you love.

Finding a workout regimen that you can stick to for the long term could be challenging. This is why it is important to participate in activities you love. Sign up for a community sport like a running club or soccer if you enjoy group sports. This would encourage you to exercise with others daily. If you enjoy solitary workouts, go for a cycle trip, a stroll, a climb, or a swim.

11. Get checked by a healthcare provider.

Suppose you are having difficulty losing weight after being active and maintaining a balanced diet. In that case, you can rule out factors that make it difficult to lose weight, such as polycystic ovarian syndrome (PCOS) and hypothyroidism. This is especially true if you have relatives that suffer from these ailments. Tell the doctor the concerns regarding this, so he or she can determine the right testing procedure to rule out any medical issues that may be causing your weight loss problems.

12. Eat a whole-foods-based diet.

Following a diet abundant in whole grains is one of the best ways to guarantee that the body receives the nutrition it needs to survive. Whole foods, such as vegetables, fruits, seeds, nuts, poultry, seafood, grains, and legumes, are high in fiber, protein, and good fats, all of which are important for maintaining healthy body weight. Whole-food-based diets, both plant-based and those containing animal products, have been related to weight reduction in various trials.

13. Eat less at night.

Many researchers have found that consuming fewer calories at night will help you sustain a healthier weight and lose unwanted fat. Over six years, those who ingested more calories at dinner were more than twice as likely to become obese than those who ate more calories earlier in the day, according to a survey of 1,245 individuals. Furthermore, people who consumed more calories at dinner were more likely to experience metabolic syndrome, a category of disorders like elevated blood sugar levels and excess belly fat. Diabetes, heart disease, and stroke are all worsened by metabolic syndrome. Breakfast and lunch can provide the bulk of the calories, so a lighter dinner could be a viable choice for weight reduction.

14. Focus on the body composition.

While your body weight is a strong indicator of fitness, body composition, including fat and fat-free mass ratios, are also important. Muscle mass, especially in older adults, is a significant predictor of optimal health. Your aim should be to add more muscle while losing weight. There are many approaches for measuring body fat levels. However, measuring the waist, calves, biceps, chest, and thighs will help you find out whether you are losing weight and adding muscle.

15. Stay hydrated in a healthy way.

Drinks with added sugars and calories, such as sweetened coffee beverages, juices, soda, sports drinks, and pre-made smoothies, are common. Sugar-sweetened drinks, particularly those sweetened with high-fructose corn syrup, have been related to weight gain and obesity, cardiac disease, diabetes, and fatty liver disease. Substituting sugary beverages for nutritious drinks like water and herbal tea will help you lose weight and lower the risk of contracting the chronic conditions listed above.

16. Choose the right supplements.

If you are exhausted and unmotivated, the right nutrients will help you get the boost you need to accomplish your goals. Your capacity to consume those nutrients reduces when you get older, raising your chance of malnutrition. Adult women over 50, for example, are often deficient in vitamin B12 and folate, two nutrients needed for energy production, according to research. B vitamin deficiencies, such as B12 deficiency, can influence your mood, discourage you from losing weight and cause fatigue. As a result, those above the age of 50 can take a high-quality B-complex vitamin to better reduce the risk of deficiency.

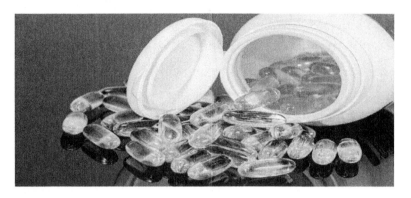

17. Limit added sugars.

For weight loss at any age, restricting foods rich in added sugar, such as sweetened drinks, candy, desserts, biscuits, ice cream, sweetened yogurts, and sugary cereals, is important. Since sugar is added to too many ingredients, even things you wouldn't believe, like salad dressing, tomato sauce, and bread, checking the product labeling is the only way to find out whether something has sugar added to it. Check for the terms "added sugars" on the nutrition facts label, or search for traditional sweeteners like high-fructose corn syrup, cane sugar, and agave in the ingredient list.

18. Improve your sleep quality.

Your weight loss efforts can be affected if you do not get sufficiently good sleep. Sleep deficiency has been related to an elevated risk of obesity and has been shown to disrupt weight loss efforts in several reports. A two-year survey of 245 women found that those who slept 7 hours or more a night were 33% more likely to lose weight than those who slept less than 7 hours a night. Weight loss progress is also related to improved sleep efficiency. Reduce the amount of light in your bedroom and stop using your cell or watching TV before bed to get the required 7–9 hours of sleep a night and boost your sleep quality.

19. Be more mindful.

Mindful eating is a simple way to strengthen your interaction with food while still helping you lose weight. Mindful nutrition entails paying closer attention to what you consume and how you eat. It helps you consider your appetite and fullness cues and how food affects your attitude and overall well-being. Many researchers have shown that practicing mindful eating techniques helps people lose weight and change their eating habits. There are no hard and quick guidelines for mindful eating, but eating gently, paying attention to each bite's taste and aroma, and keeping note of how you feel through meals are all simple ways to start mindful eating.

4.2 Beginner Exercise Programs For 50-Year-Old Women

It is never too late to start a workout regimen, whether you are 50, 65, or 80 years old. If you are new to physical exercise, though, it is a smart idea to search for a program designed specifically for beginners. Beginner fitness classes are often slower-paced and have low-impact exercises, lowering the likelihood of injuries. When browsing for a beginner's fitness routine, aim for one that includes a range of workouts, such as yoga, strength training, and aerobic activities. You will be able to practice a range of exercises to get the best out of your class this way.

Several fitness programs for women over 50 are primarily designed to assist in the growth of strength and muscle mass in this age category. Here are some of the programs listed below:

- ! **Muscles in motion**: Set the music from the 1950s and 1960s, Muscles in Motion, makes you tighten and tone the lower and upper body, emphasizing the abdominal muscles. Resistance bands, hand weights, and exercise balls are used in the group class to gain stamina.

- ! **S.O.S**: This is the exercise class for you if you are worried about the possibility of osteoporosis or bone damage. It promotes resistance workouts that improve muscle mass and bone health.

- ! **Popular Silver Sneakers®:** Silver Sneakers workout programs are available free of cost for the people on Medicare. Strength training and cardiovascular exercises are emphasized in the traditional program. Modifications are available for those who need extra help or assistance, and the program is tailored for people at all activity levels.

4.3 How Much Exercise Should You Get?

Try to aim for at least 150 minutes of moderate activity or 75 minutes of vigorous activity each week.

How much physical exercise do you get per week? The amount of exercise that is suggested for women over 50 is the same as for other adults. Per week, try to fit in at least 150 minutes of mild or 75 minutes of intense exercise. This equates to 30 minutes of moderate exercise or 15 minutes of intense exercise 5 days a week.

You should split up the workouts into short periods of time, but physicians propose that you should perform physical activity for at least 10 minutes at a time. Strengthening exercises should be done at least twice a week in addition to 150 or 75 minutes of activity.

It is also a smart idea to do balancing workouts at least three times a week if you have reduced mobility and are at risk of falling.

Before beginning a new workout regimen, one thing to keep in mind, particularly if you are new to working out, is that you get your doctor's permission before beginning any new exercise. They will also inform you of the right workouts for women above 50 and the right exercises for you, depending on the health concerns and issues.

Get out and explore while you exercise:

While attending a fitness class or working out at the local YMCA can be a great way to stay in shape while still socializing, keep in mind that you can still do your workouts outdoors. After dinner, heading out for a walk in your neighborhood can be a perfect way of seeing what is going on, getting some fresh air, and keeping the muscles healthy.

You may also take this a step further by heading for a weekend hike, which will encourage you to experience nature while also improving the stamina. Take it easy when you are first learning how to hike. Begin with short hiking on reasonably flat land. If you develop strength and confidence, you can raise the length and intensity of your hikes.

Let us take a closer look at the some of the various kinds of workouts that can help you feel better as well as some health effects of fitness for women over 50:

4.4 Best Workouts For Women Over 50

Since not all workouts are created equal, it is important to incorporate a variety of them into your fitness routine. The following are the major types of exercise that are beneficial:

! **Aerobic or cardiovascular:** Aerobic or cardiovascular workouts are also known as endurance exercises, and they must be performed for at least 10 minutes. While the breathing and pulse rate can improve through physical exercise, you can also communicate with a workout partner. Aerobic fitness includes activities such as jogging, walking, and swimming.

! **Stretching**: Stretching movements aim to enhance or retain flexibility, which decreases the likelihood of muscle or joint injury. Yoga is a well-known stretching practice.

! **Balance**: The chance of falling rises as you grow older. Falls may be reduced by doing exercises that help you develop or maintain your equilibrium. Standing on one foot may be a basic balancing workout.

Although there are many different types of exercise, it is important to remember that exercise does not happen in a void. When you exercise, for example, you are improving your cardiovascular system and strengthening your leg muscles. Any strength conditioning exercises may also be used to stretch muscles and improve balance.

Strength training: Lifting weights and workouts involving resistance, such as Pilates or resistance band workouts, are good weight training practices for women over 50. Strength and resistance training are especially important for women over 50 because they can help slow bone loss and reverse muscle loss.

3 Strength training exercises you can try at home:

Although attending a workout class at the local YMCA is a great opportunity to get out and socialize, strength training workouts may also be done from the convenience of your own home. Many of these exercises do not necessarily require the purchase of expensive machinery. You could be good to go as long as you have a couple of hand weights and chairs. A mat will help make it more convenient, but a carpeted floor will work as well.

1. Plank Pose

The plank will help you not only enhance and tone your core muscles (abdominal and lower back muscles), but it can also help you improve your equilibrium. Planks will also help you straighten your back, which benefits you if you spend much of your day seated in a desk chair. A plank could be done in a

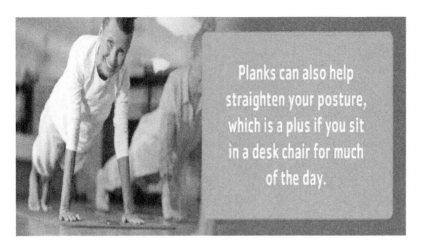

Planks can also help straighten your posture, which is a plus if you sit in a desk chair for much of the day.

variety of ways. To do a high plank, get into a stance where your arms and legs are upright as if you were at the top of a push-up. A low plank is another choice, which is simpler to do if you are a beginner. Instead of leaning on your hands, bend the arms at the elbows and lean on your forearms to sustain your weight. Keep your back perfectly straight and the head up, regardless of the version you choose. Form a straight line parallel to the floor with the whole body.

2. Squats with a Chair

Squats with a chair are another weight-bearing workout that can be done at home. Squat over a chair as if preparing to sit down, but do not contact the seat during this workout. Instead, you get back up and perform the procedure as many times as necessary. Squats will help you strengthen your balance as well as tone the lower body. When you first begin, you will notice that doing the workout with both hands and arms out in front of you is the most comfortable.

3. Chest Fly

Women's chest muscles are usually weak and underdeveloped. The chest fly is a bodybuilding exercise that makes certain muscles get stronger. You will need a couple of hand weights for this workout. Lie flat on your back on the floor, or a mat, with your knees bent and feet flat on the ground. Raise your arms over the chest with one weight in each hand. Slowly spread the arms out to the side, lowering the arms and wrists toward the ground while not touching it. Maintain a small bend in the elbows to prevent locking out the arms. Repeat with the arms raised again.

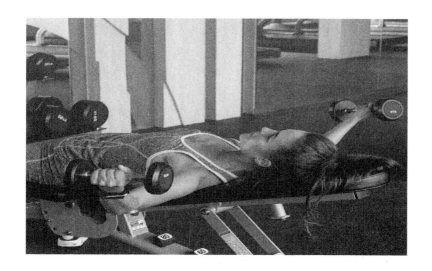

! Yoga for Women Over 50

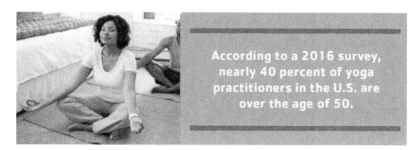

According to a 2016 survey, nearly 40 percent of yoga practitioners in the U.S. are over the age of 50.

Nearly 40% of yoga participants across the United States are over 50, as per a 2016 survey. Some people over 50 have been doing yoga for years or decades, and others are just getting started.

One thing to keep in mind about yoga is that there are various forms to choose from. Regardless of age, some types of yoga can be strenuous, too fast-paced, or physically exhausting for some individuals, while others are intended to be relaxing and gentle.

If you are a professional yogi, it is better to stick to the gentler types of yoga, emphasizing balance and stretching over muscle growth and strength.

Chair yoga is one of the easiest ways to get involved in yoga and start a fitness regimen if you have not been physically active in the past. Many of the asanas or poses in chair yoga are performed either sitting or using a seat for support while standing. Chair yoga courses are also available online.

! Swimming for Women Over 50

Swimming is one example of an excellent exercise for women over 50.

Swimming is an ideal activity for women above the age of 50. Swimming is a low-impact workout, unlike other workouts like walking and running, which can strain the joints. The water surrounds you, serving as a support and cushion, relieving pressure on your joints.

However, do not be misled by its gentleness. Swimming is a great way to have a total-body exercise. It will improve your stamina, while also developing your lower and upper body muscles, as well as your heart. Swimming will also helps improve the balance by strengthening your core, lowering your chance of falling as you return to land.

4.5 Benefits Of Exercise For Women Over 50

Age is nothing more than a figure. You may be 55, but you appear to be 40 and may sound 35. Alternatively, you may be 50 but appear and sound 65. It all comes down to how much you take care of your body and how you remain active. Many people feel that if they were not active in their twenties, thirties or forties, there is no sense in starting in their fifties or even later. Fortunately, this is not the case. It is never too late to start a workout regimen. Starting an exercise regimen will help you reverse some of the harmful consequences of inactivity while still helping you feel better about yourself.

The phrase "use 'em or lose 'em" is especially accurate when it comes to your muscles. The typical human loses around 1% of muscle a year, beginning at the age of 50. You do not have to accept muscle failure, however. Even if you are in your 90s, exercise will help you regain muscle mass. The advantages of exercise extend beyond increased muscle mass and stamina. It will also help you maintain good bone health. The body works hard to develop and build bone before you reach the age of around 30. Following that, it is more probable that you will lose bone than gain it. Because of the decrease in hormone intake, bone loss increases even more during menopause. This is when osteoporosis becomes a significant threat. However, osteoporosis and bone loss are not unavoidable. Weight-bearing workouts, which enable you to work against gravity, will boost your bone density and reduce the likelihood of bone fracture.

Let us look at some of the effects of exercise to relieve common menopause symptoms while we are on the topic of menopause. Weight gain and the growth of excess abdominal fat may occur due to the changes that occur in a woman's body during menopause, such as a decrease in hormone levels. Getting or being active during menopause will help you prevent any weight gain that comes with it. Maintaining a healthy weight will help you prevent diseases like Type 2 diabetes, cancer, and heart failure, all linked to being obese or overweight.

Chapter 5: Breakfast Recipes For Intermittent Fasting

Breakfast does not have to be difficult. These fast and easy breakfast recipes are extremely easy to make and enjoy on an intermittent fasting diet schedule with only a few ingredients. Here are some delicious and healthy breakfast recipes to start your day.

5.1 Poached eggs and avocado toast

PREP TIME: 15mins

SERVES: 4

INGREDIENTS:

! 2 ripe avocados

- ! 4 eggs

- ! 2 thick slices of bread

- ! Juice of a lime or 4tbsp lemon juice

- ! 1 cup grated edam cheese

- ! 1 tbsp freshly ground black pepper

- ! 2 tbsp salt

- ! 2 tbsp of butter to spread on the toast

DIRECTIONS:

- ! Use your general style to poach eggs.

- ! Meanwhile, take out the stones from the avocados and slice them in half.

1. Scoop the flesh into a dish or a bowl with a spoon, then add the lime or lemon juice, salt, and pepper.

2. Using a fork, mash the avocados roughly.

3. Toast some pieces of bread and spread butter on them.

4. Cover each slice of the buttered toast with the avocado mixture and a poached egg.

5. Serve immediately with a sprinkle of grated cheese.

6. You can serve fresh or fried tomato halves on each side.

5.2 Avocado quesadillas

PREP TIME: 31mins

SERVES: 2

INGREDIENTS:

- ! 1 peeled and pitted ripe avocado, chop in ¼ inch pieces

- ! 2 seeded ripe tomatoes, chop in ¼ inch pieces

- ! 1 tbsp of chopped red onion

- ! ¼ teaspoon of Tabasco sauce

- ! 2 tbsp of fresh lemon juice

- ! 1 tbsp of salt and pepper

- ! 3 tbsp of chopped fresh coriander

- ! ¼ cup of sour cream

- ! ½ teaspoon of vegetable or olive oil

- ! 24 inches of flour tortillas

- ! 1 cup shredded Monterey jack cheese

DIRECTIONS:

1. Mix the avocado, lemon juice, tomatoes, onion, and Tabasco in a small bowl.

2. Season with pepper and salt to taste.

3. Mix coriander, sour cream, salt, and pepper to taste in a separate small dish.

4. Brush the tops of the tortillas with oil and place them on a baking sheet.

5. 2 to 4 inches from the heat, broil tortillas until lightly golden.

6. Sprinkle cheese equally over tortillas and broil until melted.

7. To make 2 quesadillas, spread the avocado mixture thinly over 2 tortillas and cover it with 1 of the remaining tortillas with the cheese side down.

8. Slice the quesadillas into four wedges on a cutting board.

9. Serve warm with a spoonful of the sour cream mixture on the top of each wedge.

5.3 Mum's supper club tilapia parmesan

PREP TIME: 35mins

SERVES: 4

INGREDIENTS:

- ! 2 lbs. of tilapia fillets, red or cod snapper could be a substitute
- ! ½ cup of grated parmesan cheese
- ! 3 tbsp of mayonnaise
- ! ¼ teaspoon of salt seasoning
- ! 3 tbsp of finely chopped green onions
- ! 2 tbsp of lemon juice
- ! 4 tbsp of butter kept at room temperature

! ¼ teaspoon of dried basil

! 1 tbsp of dash hot pepper sauce

DIRECTIONS:

1. Preheat the oven to about 350 degrees Fahrenheit.

2. Arrange the fillets in a single layer in a buttered 13-by-9-inch jellyroll pan or a baking dish

3. Do not stack the fillets.

4. Apply some lemon juice on the top.

5. Mix the butter, cheese, onions, mayonnaise, and seasonings in a bowl.

6. With the help of a fork, thoroughly mix all the ingredients.

7. Bake the fish for about 10 to 20 minutes in a preheated oven or until it begins to flake.

8. Spread the cheese mixture on top and bake for 5 minutes or until golden brown.

9. The length of time it takes to bake the fish can be determined by its thickness.

10. Keep an eye on the fish to make sure it does not overcook.

Note: You can also cook the fish in the broiler.

! Broil it for about 3 to 4 minutes or before it is nearly done.

! Add the cheese and Broil for another 2 or 3 minutes, just until cheese is browned.

5.4 Avocado salad with shrimp/prawn and Cajun potato

PREP TIME: 30mins

SERVES: 2

INGREDIENTS:

! 1 tbsp of olive oil

! 300g of fresh potatoes

! Some salt to boil potatoes

! 250g or 8oz cooked and peeled king prawns

! 2 freshly sliced spring onions

! 1 minced garlic clove

- ! 1 peeled, stoned and diced avocado

- ! 2 teaspoons of Cajun seasoning

- ! 1 cup of alfalfa sprout

DIRECTIONS:

1. Cook the potatoes for about 10 to 15 minutes, or until tender, in a medium skillet of lightly salted boiling water. Drain them well.

2. In a large nonstick frying pan, skillet or a wok, heat the oil.

3. Now add the garlic, prawns, the Cajun seasoning and spring onions, and fry for about 2-3 minutes until the prawns become hot.

4. Now add the potatoes and cook for another minute.

5. Transfer to the serving dishes and top with some avocado and alfalfa sprouts before serving.

5.5 Black bean burrito and sweet potato

PREP TIME: 1hr and 5mins

SERVES: 8 to 12

INGREDIENTS:

- ! ½ teaspoon of salt

- ! 5 cups of peeled and cubed sweet potatoes

- ! 3 ½ cup of chopped onions

- ! ½ cup lightly packed cilantro leaf

- ! 2 teaspoons of vegetable oil or broth

- ! 1 tbsp of fresh minced green chili pepper

- ! 4 minced garlic cloves

- ! 4 teaspoons of ground cumin

- ! 4 ½ cups of canned black beans

- ! 4 teaspoons of ground coriander

- ! 2 tbsp of fresh lemon juice

- ! 12 flour tortillas (10 inch)

- ! 1 teaspoon of salt

- ! Fresh salsa

DIRECTIONS:

1. Preheat the oven to about 350 degrees Fahrenheit.

2. In a medium saucepan, mix the sweet potatoes, salt, and enough water to cover them.

3. Cover it and bring to a boil, then reduce to low heat and cook until the vegetables are tender for around 10 minutes.

4. Drain the water and put them aside.

5. Heat the oil in a medium saucepan or skillet and add the garlic, onions, and chile while the sweet potatoes are cooking.

6. Cover and cook them on medium-low heat, constantly stirring, for around 7 minutes, or until the onions are soft.

7. Cook while constantly stirring for another 2 to 3 minutes after adding the coriander and cumin.

8. Take the skillet off the heat and put it aside.

9. Mix the cilantro, salt, black beans, lemon juice, and cooked sweet potatoes in a food processor and make puree until smooth (or mash all the ingredients in a large bowl by your hand).

10. Add the spices and cooked onions to the sweet potato mixture in a big mixing bowl.

11. Fill each tortilla with around 2/3 to ¾ cup of the filling, roll it up, and place it seam side down in the baking dish.

12. Bake for 30 minutes, or until smoking hot while tightly covered with foil.

13. Serve with some salsa on top.

Chapter 6: Lunch Recipes For Intermittent Fasting

Are you looking for lunch ideas? If you are on an intermittent fasting diet plan, consider these meals as they are easy and nutritious lunch recipes for you to try and enjoy.

6.1 Sweet potato curry with chickpeas and spinach

PREP TIME: 30mins

SERVES: 6

INGREDIENTS:

- ! ½ cup thinly sliced sweet onions

- ! ½ tablespoon canola oil

- ! 2 teaspoons of curry powder

- ! 1 tbsp of cumin

- ! 1 teaspoon of cinnamon

- ! 10oz washed, stemmed and coarsely chopped fresh spinach

- ! 2 large peeled and diced sweet potatoes

- ! 1 can of rinsed and drained chickpeas

- ! ½ cup of water

- ! 1 can of diced tomatoes

- ! ¼ cup of chopped fresh cilantro for garnishing

- ! Brown rice or basmati rice for serving

DIRECTIONS:

- ! You can cook your sweet potatoes in whatever way you like.

- ! You can peel, slice, and steam them for around 15 minutes in a veggie steamer.

- ! Baking or boiling are both feasible choices.

- ! Heat 1-2 tsp vegetable or canola oil over medium heat as sweet potatoes are cooking.

- ! Now add the onions and cook for 2-3 minutes, or before they soften.

! Add in the cumin, curry powder, and cinnamon and stir to cover the onions in spices properly.

! Mix in the tomatoes and their juices, as well as the chickpeas, and stir to combine.

! Raise the temperature to a strong boil for around a minute or two after adding a half cup of water.

! Then, a few handfuls at a time, add the fresh spinach, stirring to cover with the cooking liquid.

! When all the spinach has been added to the pan, cover it, cook for 3 minutes, or until it is just wilted.

! Now add the cooked sweet potatoes into the liquid and stir them.

! Cook for the next 3-5 minutes, or until all the flavors are well mixed.

! Serve immediately after transferring to a serving dish and toss with some fresh cilantro.

! This recipe goes well with brown or basmati rice as well.

6.2 Grilled lemon salmon

PREP TIME: 27mins

SERVES: 4

INGREDIENTS:

- ! ½ tbsp of pepper

- ! 2 tbsp of fresh dill

- ! ½ tbsp of salt

- ! ½ lbs. salmon fillets

- ! ½ tbsp garlic powder

- ! ½ cup packed brown sugar

- ! 3 tbsp of oil

- ! 1 chicken bouillon cube mixed with 2 tbsp of water

- ! 2 tbsp of soy sauce

- ! 1 thinly sliced lemon

- ! 4 tbsp of finely chopped green onions

- ! 2 slices of onions, separated into rings

DIRECTIONS:

1. Season the salmon with dill, salt, pepper, and garlic powder.

2. Place in a small glass pan.

3. Mix the sugar, oil, chicken bouillon, green onions, and soy sauce in a large bowl.

4. Pour the mixture over the salmon and refrigerate for 1 hour, turning once.

5. Drain the marinade and toss it back.

6. Preheat the grill to medium heat and place the lemon and the onion on top.

7. Cover and Cook for 15 minutes, or until the fish is cooked properly.

6.3 The best baked potatoes

PREP TIME: 1hr and 10mins

SERVES: 1

INGREDIENTS:

- ! 1 large russet potato

- ! 1 tbsp of Kosher Salt

- ! 2 tbsp canola oil

DIRECTIONS:

- ! Preheat the oven to 350 degrees Fahrenheit and place racks in the upper and bottom thirds.

- ! Wash the potato or potatoes vigorously under cool running water with a stiff brush.

! Dry and then poke 8 to 12 some deep holes all over the spud with a regular fork to allow moisture to escape while cooking.

! Place in a bowl with a thin coating of oil.

! Season with kosher salt and put directly on the oven's middle rack.

! To collect some drippings, place a baking sheet like aluminum foil on the lower shelf.

! Bake for 1 hour, or until the skin is crisp, but the flesh underneath is tender.

! Serve by forming a dotted line with your fork from end to end, pressing the ends together to crack the spud open. It will easily open. But be alert as there will be steam.

Note: If you are cooking more than four potatoes, you will need to add up to 15 minutes to the cooking period.

6.4 Vegan fried Fish tacos

PREP TIME: 50mins

SERVES: 2

INGREDIENTS:

- ! 2 cups of panko breadcrumbs

- ! 14oz of silken tofu

- ! ½ teaspoon salt

- ! ½ cup of plain flour

- ! 1 teaspoon smoked paprika

- ! 1 teaspoon ground cumin

- ! ½ teaspoon cayenne pepper

- ! ½ cup of non-dairy milk

- ! ½ head finely shredded cabbage

- ! 2 tbsp of vegetable oil for frying

- ! 8 small tortillas

- ! 1 ripe avocado

- ! 2 tbsp vegan mayonnaise to serve

Pickled onion:

- ! 1 peeled and finely sliced red onion

- ! 1 tbsp of sugar

- ! ½ cup of apple cider vinegar

- ! 1 teaspoon of salt

DIRECTIONS:

1. To absorb extra moisture, pat the tofu with a few sheets of kitchen paper. Cut the tofu into small 1-inch pieces with a knife.

2. In a large shallow bowl, add the breadcrumbs.

3. In a separate large shallow bowl, mix the flour, smoked paprika, salt, cayenne, and cumin.

4. In a third wide shallow bowl, pour the milk.

5. Toss the tofu chunks in the flour, then the milk, then the breadcrumbs, and put them on a baking sheet.

6. Load a large frying pan with vegetable oil to a depth of 1/2 inch. Place over the medium heat and allow the oil to heat up. Fry blocks of breaded tofu until golden underneath, then turn and continue frying until golden

all over. To drain, put on a baking sheet lined with kitchen paper. Do the same for the remaining tofu.

For the pickled onion:

1. In a small kettle, heat the apple cider vinegar, salt, and some sugar until steaming.

2. Pour the hot vinegar over the thinly sliced red onion in a container or bowl.

3. Enable it to soften and turn pink, so let it sit for at least 30 minutes.

4. Serve the hot fried tofu with pickled onion, vegan mayo, avocado, and shredded cabbage in warmed tortillas. You can warm them over a lit gas ring on the stove.

6.5 Baked Mahi

PREP TIME: 40mins

SERVES: 4

INGREDIENTS:

- ! Juice of a lemon

- ! 2 lbs. of Mahi (4 fillets)

- ! 1 cup breadcrumbs

- ! 1 teaspoon salt

- ! 1 cup mayonnaise

- ! ¼ teaspoon ground black pepper

- ! ½ cup finely chopped white onion

DIRECTIONS:

1. Preheat the oven to 425 degrees Fahrenheit.

2. Place the fish in a baking dish after rinsing it. Squeeze some lemon juice over the fish, then season with salt and pepper.

3. Spread mayonnaise and sliced onions on the fish. Bake for 25 minutes at 425°F with breadcrumbs on top.

Chapter 7: Dinner Recipes For Intermittent Fasting

While doing intermittent fasting, these are the simple dinner meals you will make again and again. There is something for everyone with a variety of healthy, easy, chicken, vegetarian, and budget-friendly recipe ideas. Bon appetite!

7.1 Mediterranean chicken breast with avocado tapenade

READY IN: 15mins

SERVES: 4

INGREDIENTS:

! 1 tbsp of grated lemon peel

! 4 skinless and boneless chicken breast halves

- ! 2 tbsp of olive oil

- ! 5 tbsp of fresh lemon juice

- ! 1 finely chopped garlic clove

- ! ¼ teaspoon of ground black pepper

- ! ½ teaspoon salt

- ! 2 roasted and mashed garlic cloves

- ! ¼ fresh ground pepper

- ! ½ teaspoon sea salt

- ! 1 seeded and finely chopped medium tomato

- ! 3 tbsp of rinsed capers

- ! ¼ thinly sliced cup of small green pimento stuffed olive

- ! 1 finely chopped Hass avocado

- ! 2 tbsp of finely sliced fresh basil leaves

DIRECTIONS:

1. Combine chicken, 2 tablespoons of lemon juice, lemon peel, 2 tablespoons of olive oil, salt, garlic, and pepper in a sealable plastic bag. Refrigerate for approximately 30 minutes after sealing the bag.

2. Combine the remaining 3 teaspoons lemon juice, 1/2 teaspoon olive oil, sea salt, roasted garlic, and freshly

ground pepper in a mixing bowl. Mix the basil, green olives, tomato capers, and avocado and set them aside.

3. Remove the chicken from the bag and pour out the marinade. Grill for about 4 to 5 minutes per side over medium-hot coals or until the optimal degree of doneness is achieved.

4. Avocado Tapenade is a great addition to serve with this dish.

7.2 Vegan lentil burgers

READY IN: 1hr and 10mins

SERVES: 4

INGREDIENTS:

! 2 ½ cups water

! 1 cup well rinsed dry lentils

- ! ½ teaspoon salt

- ! ½ diced onion

- ! 1 tbsp of olive oil

- ! 1 diced carrot

- ! 1 tbsp of soy sauce

- ! 1 teaspoon pepper

- ! ¾ cups finely ground rolled oats

- ! ¾ cup breadcrumbs

DIRECTIONS:

1. Lentils should be cooked for 45 minutes in salted water. The lentils would be soft, and much of the moisture would have evaporated.

2. In a small amount of oil, fry the onions and carrots until tender, approximately for 5 minutes.

3. Combine the cooked ingredients, soy sauce, pepper, oats, and breadcrumbs in a bowl.

4. Shape the mixture into patties when it is still warm; it will produce 8-10 burgers.

5. After that, the burgers can be shallow fried for about 1-2 minutes on each side or bake for 15 minutes at 200°C.

7.3 Brussel sprout and sheet pan chicken

READY IN: 40mins

SERVES: 4

INGREDIENTS:

- ½ cup Brussels sprouts

- 4 skin-on chicken thighs

- 3 tbsp of olive oil

- 4 carrots, cut on the bias

- 1 tbsp of herb de Provence

DIRECTIONS:

1. Preheat the oven to 400 degrees Fahrenheit.

2. Put 11/2 tbsp olive oil, 12 tsp herbs, pepper, and salt in a bowl and add the cut vegetables. Rub the vegetables all over.

3. Arrange the vegetables on a sheet pan.

4. In the same bowl, place the chicken thighs. Drizzle with 1/2 tablespoons herbs, 1/12 tablespoons olive oil, and season with salt and pepper. Rub the chicken all over.

5. Place the chicken in the pan.

6. Roast for 30-35 minutes, or until chicken is cooked through.

7. Switch the oven to broil and roast for a minute or two and if you want a crispier chicken skin or crispier vegetable. If you do not keep an eye on it, it can burn, so watch carefully.

7.4 Crock pot black-eyed peas

READY IN: 1hr and 5mins

SERVES: 6

INGREDIENTS:

1 bag of 16oz dried black-eyed peas

1 small ham hock

1 can of Del Monte zesty jalapeno pepper

1 can of diced tomato with green chilies

2 cans of chicken broth 1 chopped stalk celery

DIRECTIONS:

1. Pre-soak the black-eyed peas according to the instructions given on the bag.

2. Mix all the ingredients and cook on low medium flame for about 1 hour.

3. Serve with white rice.

7.5 Brocolli dal curry

READY IN: 1hr and 30mins

SERVES: 4

INGREDIENTS:

- ! 4tbsp of butter or 4 tbsp of ghee

- ! 2 chopped onions

- ! 1 tbsp of chili powder

- ! 1 ½ teaspoon of black pepper

- ! 2 tbsp of cumin

- ! 1 teaspoon ground coriander

- ! 2 teaspoons turmeric

- ! 1 cup red lentil

- ! Juice of a lemon

- ! 3 cups chicken broth

- ! 2 finely chopped medium broccoli

- ! ½ cup dried coconut

- ! 1 tbsp of flour

- ! 1 teaspoon of salt

- ! 1 cup of coarsely chopped cashews

DIRECTIONS:

1. In a saucepan, melt the butter and brown the onions.

2. Now add the pepper, chili powder, cumin, coriander, and turmeric.

3. And stir and cook for a minute.

4. Add the lemon juice, lentils, broth, and coconut.

5. Bring to a boil, reduce to low heat, and cook for 45-55 minutes (if the mixture becomes thick, you have to add a little hot water).

6. Now steam the broccoli for approximately 7min.

7. Set aside broccoli after submerging it in cool water.

8. Remove 1/3 cup of the liquid from the lentil mixture.

9. To make a smooth paste, add in the flour.

10. Return it to the pan and mix in the salt, broccoli, and nuts.

11. Cook for 5 minutes on low heat.

12. Serve with basmati rice.

Conclusion

Rather than a traditional diet, the intermittent fasting diet plan is a way of eating. An intermittent fasting diet emphasizes when you eat, rather than what you eat as per conventional diet plans. You alternate through cycles of extreme or full-calorie restriction, in other terms, periods of fasting and healthier eating while following this eating style. The duration of these calorie-restricted and healthy-eating cycles differs according to one's personal desire.

Intermittent fasting (IF) is one of the most famous health and fitness phenomena in the world right now. People are using it to lose weight, boost their health, and ease their lives. Intermittent fasting is also a very easy and effective lifestyle approach. During a fast, several people report feeling healthier and gaining more energy. Furthermore, intermittent fasting also lowers the risk of developing certain chronic diseases. Intermittent fasting helps you consume and enjoy a broad range of foods because it does not restrict which foods to eat and which to skip, instead it focuses on a well-balanced, nutrient-dense diet. Many studies have shown that it may have a significant impact on the body and brain and that it can also help you live longer. According to the International Food Information Council (IFIC), about 10% of more than 1,000 Americans aged 18 to 80 who were surveyed in early April practice intermittent fasting, making it one of the most popular lifestyles. The way we eat food to sustain our fitness, performance, and recovery becomes more important as we get older. Good eating is easy, but it may be hard to manage and maintain. A woman's health declines tremendously during her pre-menopausal and post-menopausal phases. Their living standard suffers as a result of this. As intermittent fasting is a code to longevity, the intermittent fasting diet plan is structured in such a way that your body can remain balanced while fasting and even increase your life span. So, with a few supportive workouts and certain dietary options, check out this fantastic lifestyle approach, as intermittent fasting is an excellent way to reduce serious health conditions that women often face in their late 40s. As a result, this book is a must if you want to improve your fitness and longevity. You are not going to be disappointed.

Printed in Great Britain
by Amazon

63446002R00071